The Season's V
New and Sel

Sheri Benning grew up on a small
She has since travelled widely while attaining several academic degrees. Benning is the author of two collections of poetry, *Thin Moon Psalm* (Brick Books) and *Earth After Rain* (Thistledown Press), but this is her first collection to be published in the UK. Her poetry, essays and fiction have also appeared in numerous Canadian and British literary journals and anthologies, including *New Poetries V* (Carcanet, 2011). Benning divides her time between Glasgow, where she completed her PhD, and her family's farm near Manitou Lake, Saskatchewan.

Also by Sheri Benning

Tag: Canadian Poets at Play, co-editor
(Fernie, BC: Oolichan Books, Autumn 2015)

Thin Moon Psalm (London, Ontario: Brick Books, 2007)

Earth After Rain (Saskatoon: Thistledown Press, 2001)

SHERI BENNING

The Season's Vagrant Light

New and Selected Poems

CARCANET

First published in Great Britain in 2015 by

Carcanet Press Limited
Alliance House
Cross Street
Manchester
M2 7AQ

www.carcanet.co.uk

We welcome your comments on our publications
Write to us at info@carcanet.co.uk

A CIP catalogue record for this book is available from the British Library

ISBN 978-1-78410-106-0

The publisher acknowledges financial assistance from Arts Council England

Typeset by XL Publishing Services, Exmouth
Printed and bound in England by SRP Ltd, Exeter

Contents

From *Earth After Rain*

From *Thin Moon Psalm*

New Poems

From *Earth After Rain*

Why I'm Afraid to Have Children

Because my bones are doors that enclose you and your arrival will unhinge me. I will dislocate, a tectonic shift.

Because my belly will distend and after I will be a hollow mollusk, streamed with seaweed.

Because your heart is a hummingbird in a nest of filament veins.

Because I might drop you on my scabby linoleum floor as when I dropped my grandmother's crystal vase, everywhere prismatic shards.

Because I am 22
                    I am 42
                                        I am 35. Because I would rather give up my life than my self and you will demand no less.

Because a vampire, who teaches high school during the day, lives in the apartment below my boyfriend's. Late at night little girls file into his lair like animals facing slaughter. When I pass them in the hall, they cover their faces, their hands the colour of yellowing pearls.

Because the pain of your descent hovers like a wasp and my mother who told me I'll forget has been known to lie.

Because the river is veiled by iridescent skin that conceals a current. Because pregnant women's skin, which is said to glow, conceals what might drown them.

Because your fingertips are wild strawberries, crushable and then sweet bud-blood.

Because I heard that pregnant women in Nazi war camps had their legs tied together and I don't want to know how this could kill me.

Because while sunbathing on a beach last summer I saw a sail, small as your first tooth.

You're like that sail floating on an inland sea. The closer we get, the bigger you become –

Under the Noon Moon

Yesterday at the doctor's, my x-rayed hips,
the cave we pass through, what lovers enter into,
what I will look like after years in the earth.

Now, under the noon moon, a shed clover seed,
dried blood of roseberries, blueberries, frost-split skins,
speargrass goldenrod, sun stirred by poplars,
molasses heat on my flannelled shoulders –

I stumble on pelvic-curled driftwood and remember
my bone's glow sifting dirt. Squall of leaving geese,
thousands of sun-white bellies jerking on the river's
waves, comforts me the way a parent does a child
and the child needs no proof.

Bear Letter #1

Bear,

If I continue to walk this path of sinking light
we will meet. Drawn by tides of shadow,
a huffed poplar seed sucked by lake.

Wood asphodels, rooted constellations, guide me.
The forest is thick with your dank gravity,
a woman-weight moments before birth.

Sun, a wild rose rotting. Tendrils of last light
tangled in twigs. Birds flit, heartbeats –
poplar leaf shadows.

I wear your loamy incense:
moss, sloughed poplar bark,
blue undertones of moon and rain.

Bear, I don't know how
this will end.

Bear Letter #2

Bear,

I have never given birth,
my womb a spring plum.
But Bear, you teach me birth,
your name a verb, muscles river-roll
over your bones as you hunker.
Your holler, guttural.
Earth tears beneath your paws.

Birthing room, a cave, ice-white walls.
Hibernation over, you hunger-howl.
You are beside   inside
coming out –
                    You burrow through a leaf shadow,
emerge from a labium shrouded by
shavegrass, ragweed, passionflower.
Your fur slick with symbiotic
swamp you left behind. Hunger-howl –
nipples, sun-hard chokecherries.

Everywhere your fetid musk:
cracked skin   marsh root
blood   moss   scat.

Bodies of Stones

Measure the distance
they've come, wear river
and bitter rain. In lacunas
of night-breath we learn
to hold each other –
before words
or after.

Blind

Through every thing we love, light comes in. Love, an aperture, shows the world in new ways. The curve of the ear whispered into when night lays down on you, like sun through rain-sequined sky.

That is why we are disoriented when love leaves. Having lost a way of focus, all sight becomes peripheral.

When my head was on your chest, filled with the ocean sounds of blood, July sky was a bulging vein. Air above pavement serpentine as Latin dancers. Elm leaves, embossed by the bronze dusk sun, flicked at the moment light's slow tickle became unbearable – tails of jut-ribbed horses. Later we smelled of grass, a lover's lingering scent, hair woven into a shirt.

But now snow falls soft and random, the ohs and ahs of bodies entwined.

Not love, but its absence, makes us blind.

The Night was Split

How the night was split
by stars cat-teeth sharp
and the moon stiff as a swan
feather, how you passed out
at some party and woke to
him on you, a nest of blood,
sweat and hair, his pounding
between your legs reminding
you of waves against the pier
where you sat last October in
pigeon sound and the yellow
smell of death and shit

and how he must have bit
off your tongue, a fish
beached in sun,
because only now
can you tell me –
voice a sparrow's
flight in wind –
of the blood,
the stars,
the night
split.

That Ugly Thing

My friend in the psych ward cries unless she's asleep.
Her room dark, a mouth silenced. Nurses bring paper-cups
of neon-sweet pills that make her forget she feels

ugly. Last week, my Dad dragged a dead fox
out from under my cabin. For a day I watched it
peripherally, caught pink glimpses of its lulled tongue.

When my friend was sixteen a man tore into her.
And just as wheat sprouts where a farmer shakes
out his overalls, a husk split in her womb.

Three months later, blood-sopped petals.
Secrets make a gravity. It pulls on you
until you can't stand. She told no one.

I want to look at the fox, touch its eyes, black as what fire
leaves behind, but only a smear remains. Dad hauled it away,
'Didn't want you to have to look at that ugly thing.'

The World Open

Tears make you believe
you are underwater.
Pines seaweed-sway
and the moon wears
the shape of waves.

Mom's heart stops
and all time shifts.
The four-hour drive
to the hospital – days.

•

Our night car travels the terrain of a cave:
pines, stalagmites, stars, bat eyes, night air,
leathery skin. My fingers through the window
brush wings and I think it's wind.

•

In the glow of his cigarette, my father's flesh drips,
leaves from November poplars.
My father points at death, its smoulder,
the tip of his cigarette, in the cave of my belly.

Before my brother left to study
we went to a pub.
Despite the pull of beer, he gave us names
for muscles and veins.
The feel of Latin on our skin,
sounding out each pore.

Without him to translate,
the doctor's words hover –
a cyclone of bees.
Lack of language
makes us involuntary.
My sister grabs my hand.
Magma-heat, her beating blood.

•

As children we learned tectonic plates
balance on pools of stone. Tides of heat
tear earth apart. Under winter skies,
my siblings and I drawn by heat
into our parents' bed, a web of limbs.
Ears pressed to chests, we hear
the world open. Continents remember
Pangaea by the bend in their bodies.
My cheekbone defines the curve of mom's hand.

My Body That Is For You

Anthony Benning

Earth sucks his body like a seed,
frees him from an oiled wood
and velvet husk.

Rhizomes bloom in empty eye-nooks.
Bread broken by wrung hands,
evergreen roots. They braid

his leaven bones. Blood and flesh feed
fingertip-sized nodes. He pulses
in flame-shaped pine cones.

Impossible Endings

Last night I watched you lean over your mother.
Hospital light washed you in water-colour.
Your body's shadow, stained sedge, definitions
of endings, impossible. You told me once
we all come from the same DNA. We all pass
through the hips of a familiar mother.

•

At the equinox they sedate her.
Outside, wheat sates new hunger.
A sharp moon decrescendos.
Earth waits open.

•

The night she dies you rest
your head in the hollow
between my breasts.
Heartbeat, careless
wing thrum. Heartbeat,
a sound you can carry
in a teaspoon.

From *Thin Moon Psalm*

Listen

Fall. The season of listening for what we must let go. But your listening was something hungry, a demand to be spoken to. To be heard. Now far from him you remember two things. Probably accidents or undeserved gifts. Like the slant way you realize Spring – weak-tea light of dusk, wrist's moon-shadow when you hold the hot cup. A knowing that slinks through your gaze. But you're doing it again. Please. Just listen.

Driving him to work. Morning moon passing through pine – sleight of hand, shocks of silver. The story of the farrowing sow. How as a kid he sat in the broth of straw, burnt wood, manure. Furious mewing, steaming birth, he'd place the litter in a box of rags, cut their teeth, return them to their mother. How he and his brothers took turns waiting. Head wrapped in scarves of sleep, he'd break the night-mirror, split light of snow-stars pooled in alloy sky. How he sang stories to stay awake.

You realize you are panicking. You want to free him from the scars of smoke, work, whisky, that tear him from the small songs he made in front of the fire where he learned how to wait.

Listening has made your heart a bruise, a dark pearl of gravity. Outside your cabin, the great blue heron rising each morning, a gesture of abandonment to what is more. It shames you. You watch the moon finally sink into a barbed crown of unlit pine and not rise. That's the only thing you can recall with any sort of clarity – the moon's last time and with such voiceless ease.

What It Tastes Like

(Hoarfrost)

In near-dark,
when she's almost
asleep. Smell of coming
rain, wet wool. A spore
of the farm rises in her.
Animals, shadow-pulse.
Her father in the barn.
Rubber boots. Manure.
Open door cedar-light.
Kitchen window weeping
the beet soup loam, sweat
of someone you love. Hands
thick with work and cold
around a hot bowl. Autumn
dusk in bled cloud – loose
straw, spilled oil, a concrete floor.
Steam's in-between-breath pause.
Stars, tin, a drink of well-water.

As when you pull a stone from the river,
and hold it in your palm. The light is wrong.

Filleting

Time redeemed through memory is emotional reality.
Larry Benning, study notes on *Four Quartets*, 1967

Pike guts, motor oil, milky coffee, birch sap,
passing me flesh on knife-tip, fish scales
stuck to palm – scatter-light,
unfocused eyes,

Well it was a Heidt from St Gregor. Big sonofabitch. I was drinking at the Burr bar by myself and he starts up with me. Oh you know – 'think you're so smart' – shit like that. And I don't want to fight but you know how it is, so we head outside. And I get the jump on him. Mushed his face pretty good. You know slim guys like me gotta do it hard and do it first. And he starts bawling – bloody embarrassing. So I pick him up and haul him to the john – through the back so no one has to see – and I help him clean up. Then I buy him a beer and I tell him to leave me the fuck alone. Well shit, then the sonofabitch's uncle starts up with me and he's a big bloody bastard and I'm not there to fight so I just buy a six-pack to take home. But of course he follows me out so I just set the beer in the truck box. And he starts dancing around, thinks he's Cassius Clay, so I ask him if he wants to dance or fight and he keeps hopping like an ignorant asshole so I kick him a little – just so he'd drop his hands – and then I plough him one something furious. And the silly sonofabitch leaned in or something so damned rights I get him right between the eyes. The poor bugger walked around with two black eyes for a helluva long time. Anyway, Wilf Chernetsky and them other guys they came to break it up then but I just left. I guess that Meyer kid who works at the butcher shop was there. And well shit – next thing he's telling everybody in the countryside how I beat up both those big sonofabitchin Heidts –

left lid memory-pinched, flexed jaw, pose
for the deep-bellied 'huh', the hang-time vowel
between a story's end and the meaning of it all.
You want him to blink, to shake his head, but

goddamn bunch of bullshit.

He doesn't move.

What Passes Through

November sky: a mouth
that has smoked too much for years. Cold

that could make you bleed, thin
whistle of sun.

Running on scabbed ice. Poplar death,
familiar smell of what passes through dark:

menses   breath   sweat.

That time of day when the membrane
that keeps us separate begins

to fray – sudden rip of the heart,
wolf-flick on the back of the eye.

Errata? Look again. Only the sky's
gaunt skin, but I saw something.

Womb

: petal-curled in the garden of my mother,
beneath the moth-drone of her lungs, in her

wish and blood; before my voice became
descent; before language, the sound of distance

between what is divided –

every word I say, traced back to first exile;
every word, rooted in parting; every word

is echo for that moth-drone,
that wish, that blood.

Torn Flesh

'in dead earnest offer the betrayed world a rose'
Zbiegniew Herbert

I want to write how
my lover's eyes imply

a boy from Haiti

a good harvest, a winter of full-
bellied dream, how his eyes

died today,

are a currency that no longer purchases:
penny, kopeck, half-moons

hatchet deep

of clay under fingernails, horse-hooves,
elm-bark, how

in his flesh

lying at night in the willow nest of his rib-cage,
next to his corvine heart,

until he was no more,

I lean into the silty river of his gaze,
see my face reflected –

a shred of local news –

to say is only to weave
torn flesh, *bright and*
bloody rags in the dark.

Sleeping Blue

The night before I leave there is a storm. Wind, a train
down Nevsky that runs past us before we can turn
to see what it is. Street dirt bites our eyes,
sunset culled by fists of cloud.

We undress, hold each other urgently; heat of our bodies
a false certainty. Tired and dumb, we whisper small words,
I love you, I love you, pebbles to dam the tide of coming morning.
Forgive us. We don't know how. Love is not inevitable –

when we meet what can't be named, that we choose to love
is a kind of grace that shades everything. Like the soft shadows
of night-snow turning winter into a sleeping-animal blue.

In the morning we take a cab to the airport.
Sky, a bloodless face we can't read; suspect it might be judging us.
We think we might've lacked courage the night before,
though we don't say.

Sometimes I will dream of return, but in the dreams clouds entropy.
Wind shears your face. And instead of coming home with bread
and wine
to find me reading at our kitchen table, a candle gutters
and you will walk away.

At the airport we sit on the steps, share a cigarette.
Without thinking you reach over to wipe something from my lip,
hold your finger there. Later you help me carry my bags through
customs,
yell an insult back at the guards before you kiss each of my eyelids,

and promise we'll meet soon. Forgive us, we lack courage.
Don't know how to hold the pose of letting go. But the grace
of the moment on the step, your finger pressed to my lip,
its small shadow – a sleeping-animal blue.

October Light:

i

Not the flute-song light of April,
of skittish creak waves or
the heart-in-throat jitter
of aspen leaves.

ii

When you peel back the husk.

iii

Allspice, cinnamon, unwashed hair,
cloves pinned to over-ripe oranges,
sweat of yesterday's labour.

iv

Doesn't turn around though it can feel the eyes at its back.

v

Nor is it November's slag-light, the thing said
by a lover that cannot be taken back and now sits
between them, broken-winged and awkward.
Not light of the thin cough after.

vi

Inward light –
viscous magma, lamp in a night window,
light of a thought you can't yet say, blood, embers
through the seams of an old wood-stove. Light that invites,
go deeper.

viii

A thick-tongued drunken prophet, light
that spills long shadows at your feet as if to slur.
It knows how to come to grips with the darkness
that is coming, but it's not going to say.

Lastochka

9 May 2002

•

To watch the Victory Day fireworks
we join the crowd walking down Nevsky Prospekt to Palace Square –
faces blend together, blank as stars.

While he buys us beer from a kiosk, I listen.
Some men clustered round guitars.
Mandel'štam believes something as fine as
                                        a flute can pull us from our prisons,
        can piece together disarticulated days,

but these men strum furiously.
Veins bulging, they shout their songs –

                                              all of the cocked triggers
of all the executions during the siege. When he returns,
I reach for his hand,
                    his pulse fine as the curled syllables
his mother calls him – *lastochka,*
small sparrow.

•

The winter before, *dikaya radost'*:
his shoulder-first walk
into Nevsky's light-soaked snow.

Dikaya radost': I learned to balance words
on teeth and tongue. Diphthongs
subtle as the western meadowlark back home.

Dikaya radost': descent into the strata of the heart,
that old city labyrinth. At each turn a talisman – two pigeons
on my sill, dawn-grey; their refracted coo, light through water.

Dikaya radost': untranslatable as children
shucking the day's weight,
their utter, feral joy.

Now, though, difference
in how I hold him –
my arms a basket, open.

•

Poetry shakes, says Mandel'štam, a lover's hand pulls us
out of sleep. We wake in the middle of a word,
                                        a crystal room, where love also means
forcing your child onto a train for Pskov or Novgorod.
Mother-songs, charms in tuliped fists
of children fed to squalls of German soldiers.

We wake where war means a few pieces of bread a day. No heat.
How people survived the Nazi siege
like night-rats –

We wake where sun is a word rising
                                        from the dead; poems, stones
unearthed from the memories of friends. And *govorit'*, to speak,
means to be always waking.

•

He stood at our kitchen-window while I boiled water for tea. Soon
we'd both return to reading, but for a moment,
in the slow exhale of late afternoon,

he was caught by the absent-minded clouds and the saw-toothed
February
wind lifting sodden papers, corners of skirts, in the courtyard. I
turned away
from the stove –

on the sill, a rained-on book,
Gogol's *Dead Souls*, which he translated for me –
a lone note of music tries to express bliss
but in its own echo hears emptiness.
Maybe, he thought, despair.

Stunned by
the barbed cry of a gull,
the imprecision of speech,
how a single word would rip this
light like steam,
my tongue,
a broken wing.

•

bwili noche:

Spare light of a sun –
it won't look away while the city undresses –
fallen edges, shadow-silk strewn on cobblestone.
Rain-freed smell of lilacs, willow-sap; blade of moon,
grass caught on river-skin, a shiver

in half-lit sky. When he came into the kitchen
to tell me about Shostakovich's art –
to transcend,

one must bear witness – I thought about Rodin's counsel:
travailler, rien que travailler.
Standing on a quay
in the Neva's alkaline breath, Rilke practiced
how to not look away –

Russia, he thought, ever-changing, never defined,
a growing God;
to bear witness, we must transcend ourselves.

Outside the sun still
stooped on candle stubs,
the broken city
horizon. Its thorns of light tore my eyes –
bone-light of sky
slow cry of the contrite,
rain.

•

polnoch':

half-night. Whetstone
for my own word. Midnight
might not be distance measured,
a pilgrim in the middle of a journey,
but a nearing lack or whole. Sky,
a tense blue

song of balance, a voice that could, at any moment,
fall. I wanted to tell him about watching the city pull away
from a boat on the Neva, faceless buildings, embers,
surprised by the city's existence outside of my own.
Like the first time I discovered my mother

in old letters from a lover. I was ashamed then
as when I watched the old soldiers dancing with the folk-singers

under the arch of Palace Square. The waver of their shadow-lank
limbs, the tense beauty of watching what could, at any moment,
fall. The crowd I was voyeur to sung words I recognized
but had not lived.

                              The scene reminded me of *Sacrifice*,
the Čiurlionis painting: lamb-smoke when suffering is oblation,
visible only when the city pulled away, but the confused shadows
of bodies cleaved, the folk-song's minor key still vibrating in the arch,

                              bray without release. I wanted to tell him
but could not. The word 'sacrifice' a lie if I spoke aloud.
Something I hadn't considered before.

Polnoch':
          nearing lack; nearing whole

•

In the looseness of March we walked back
from The Idiot, a basement restaurant named
after the novel. Along the Neva I thought:
                              crocus petals, willow catkins, brome; mouth

sticky with memory, the wet clothes that drown,
my sadness lit
          by distance, by belief

in the whole vowel, home. We scried
the mess on the Neva –
                                    soaked city light, river-weed, wraiths

of almost remembered dreams. We said our stories
how we wished they could be.
                                    The way they never were.
Conscience a wet cold that invades bones.

Remember that painting by Ge?
        Seed-scatter of early stars and Judas in the shadow of a crowd.

Moon, a bloodless hand, rises up his back,
lights his weight.

•

Sheathed in salt-sky the sun is the shape of your shock –
awed eye.

How to say the sun over the Neva before
tallow-lit dusk?

Only upon failing to name can we open to loss.
The sun, a moment in time

transcends time. The landmark dissolves in our blood, tallow-lit
dusk,

and somewhere remains whole –

like that cross in the ditch, toothed by wind,
that was always half-way home.

•

Palace Square. Victory Day. Sky, a grave
containing us all. I reach for his hand
to curl up in the small shadow of his pulse,
but the air shatters,
a fight rips past me – students, skinheads.

A kid wearing orange Doc Martens falls and
one of the skinheads kicks him,
breaks his skull.

Someone cries *You bastard*
air tears open:
the skinheads scatter, the dying kid's friends scream
for the militia, for an ambulance.

I land on the pavement, head between my knees;
legs convulse, the orange boots jerk.
I can't look.

Mandel'štam asks us
does the skull unfold –
temple to temple – so that armies, their soldiers, can flow
through our eyes?

Hymn

Oh morning moon,
your exiled limp –

spine-bent, eye-on-earth, shedding
yourself along the way. As if

your thinning gaze could ever end
in return. As if the basin of ache

you leave, fossa beneath the braid
of breastbone, could ever be assuaged.

•

slipped

from earth's pocket,
the stone you pulled

from the shore, forgot
you had, but miss

when you crave something
exact. When the space between

your curled finger and thumb
is a small sadness you want

to fill rather than
look through –

•

Before we knew your weightlessness,
we did not know how hard

we fall. Unaware of gravity,
time is meaningless; time, the measure

of gravity's gait. Loss of you
is the beginning of speech. Before

there was no need to forage
words, no forest-shadow

of gasped pine,
cried-out leaves.

•

Oh morning moon,
grandmother's arm

waned by holding water.
Your slow descent

into silence
we call new

shows us our own
slow descent into loss

is birth.

Bird Bones

Air screamed through your bird-bones as you flew
from your snowmobile, into a field of snow and stubble,

once an inland sea. Your spine unhinged.
I stand around the corner of your hospital room,

Andrew, listen to my father sing as he holds your quivering legs.
What emerges from our bodies cracked open? The stiff door

of an abandoned farmhouse: orbit of dust,
flurry of dark wings. Propelled

by the thrum of your heart you landed
in a prairie of frozen stars, my father's song –

the one he sang to me when I fell here, heart-first
and screaming, into the sudden rush of sky.

Descent from the Cross, Rembrandt, 1634[1]

Hermitage Museum, St Petersburg, Russia

---

1 The face in the Rembrandt of the man pulling Christ off the cross. It's my father pacing from the machine shed to the barn. Night diffuse with the silence of *I have nothing*. Empty-arm begging of autumn fields beneath sky. Dry snow – flaked stars, moths of reflected light. Wheat two bucks a bushel. Harvest dust-thin. His body a reed flexed with work and frost. In the middle of his life, a grief that stops blood.

In the painting, a woman holds a candle. The worn-cotton glow of the yardlight poorly cloaking the back of night. The man pulling Christ off the cross is thinking nothing. Not *What should I do? What should I do?* because to look it in the eye is to die. He's just standing, now in the barn, the heat of sleeping breath, straw, manure. His bloodless face drifts in the cadence of animal-pulse. Across his shoulders a burlap sack of feed. Against his cheek, silence where a heart once beat.

Thin Moon Psalm

Monastery of Christ in the Desert, New Mexico

'*...life consists of love, languor, sweetness, heat and melody...*
a 13th C. Carthusian Mystic

Wet-feather
moon, half-

sunk in
sun-

frayed
rice grass

world without -

•

bone-curved
morning incense

Kyrie

rises in the valley – chamisa,
false mallow, pinyon pine.

eleison

dizzy moon, thin with sorrow-
light, falls beneath dawn

Christe

•

the shape of hunger ~

Sun-sucked cholla cactus
hull, a many-moth gray.

Where once it drew blood, flute-slits,
hollow smell of heat and weeds.

Later, this is what your voice,
your eyes, what you use in hunger

to enter others,
will be.

•

gutted ~

The valley unfolds along the river-spine.
You stutter through a maze of desert-

parsley, ice smell of juniper,
wolf-eye-green sage.

Skulls and clay, held in flex
by the weight of time, wear wind-veins.

Thirst throbs on the dark drum, a fire-flower
in the mouth cave, syncopated to the snake heat-hum –

what is wet inside you wants to escape,
to be oblation for the sun.

What is wet inside wants to shuck you –
the gutted sandbar willow, a shed pod,

ecstatic branches of praise.

•

what scares you ~

Moth clenched
on the morning door.
Last night, drone of moon-

leaf wings in exhaled air.
Desire convulsive

but precise. Now the moth
grips with the silence that holds
stone together.

•

that song that goes ~

Listen
to the Chama river
carry mountains
on its back:

this is the wood
of the cross –

come,
worship.

•

going ~

You come to a desert to know
but leave with only rinds of clay,
throat full of psalms,

rain-hush of monks sweeping,
straw on stone. The Chama River,
heaving coyote whine, cragged-light,

finds ocean, does not stay.
Somewhere a man heaves us
on his shoulders. Eyes sliced

by a million mirrors, sun on sand.
He still falls to knuckled rock
we cannot know;

there's only going,
straw on stone.

Fidelity

'At last the fidelity of things opens our eyes.'
Zbigniew Herbert

Once my sister was sick. So much over which she had no say
had happened to her body; it lay dormant in her sinew for years.

Then, the aftershock –

I sat beside her when they slipped her body into the MRI.
I wanted to hold her, I prayed

as though I was a pauper willing to trade up
glass-beads and feathers, something as useless as my life,

for her safety. That night driving in Saskatoon,
she didn't believe the moon could look like it did.

I drove her to the edge of the city's halo. Hemmed in
by wheat and barley, glow of a bare-bulb in the root-cellar

of August dusk. We hung our heads out the car windows
into cricket hum. Stars. And there it was –

moon, a cupped palm, sallow,
and ready to receive.

What It Tastes Like

(Salt)

In the smeared light
of a hardware store,
urine smell, burning
coffee. Against some hip,
the dead-leaf crush of a diaper.
It rises in her. Shadows
threshed by noon sun
implying nothing. A fly
in a bowl of bloated cereal,
sweet milk. Jack-in-the-box
cartoon-caw, a TV left on
a room away. Her father
in a harrow-cloud of brittle
earth. Lilacs, like swollen
lips, in a jam jar. Yesterday's
boiled potatoes. Carrots
in the sink. Metal
taste of dirt. Her mother
in the kitchen, crying.

Her body won't forget. Ridge of skin
after the sloughing of a scab.

Dance

My brother wakes me to tell me about his night: breath,
whisky, smoke, starred, December sky. How he danced

with a woman the way I once showed him –
he too misses a body scarred by the same steep

path of birth. Now we live a country apart.
Dancing together is rare. Slow hum of heat

echoes the shape of him, lifts me
from a dream of drowning in that creek

west of our farm, where our thirst for return
began, the fetal glow of my face in reeds –

I refuse to let go of the home
we were cast from so I can begin

to breathe. His clove breath,
starred sky, echo of heat,

tell me of night. Now we live
a country apart; dancing is rare.

He wakes me to forgive me
for believing my despair

is like no other despair.

Sing

Glass rain of pigeon song
beneath a bridge spanning the Saint John River –
I don't know how to be here.

Remember last summer?
The autistic boy singing *oh oh oh* running
circles around his tent he became what he thought.

Far away now, you believe if your gaze could lie
in the father arms of fallow fields, the dull hunger of November
sky, it could rest. Home defined by circles of thought.

In the shards of another's song, remember
the autistic boy's *oh oh oh*. Your own
empty-pocket refrain.

November Light

i

November light, without a home –
back-bent on the corner of Whyte and 105th
in a torn jean-jacket, cigarette-smoke grey, muttering
at passersby about the darkness coming.
Few listen. Few even turn their heads.

ii

Light of that pig fetus in the dusty quart jar
at the back of the grade 10 Biology cupboard.

iii

Afraid to open your mail? Shadows
under your eyes? When you think,
do you just get sad?

iv

Not October light, the whisky-jack drunk
on fermented crabapples dancing in the dying
flames of the apple tree.

v

Of bone-ash and clay,
which harden into something that can shatter.
If you must, speak in hushed tones.

vi

The doe's coat turns dun so she can hide
in spaces cut by bare aspen branches near
the Saskatchewan River. Only her wet-eyed stare
is visible. November light, something unseen
watching.

Bones in the Wings

When he kissed me between my shoulder blades,
I thought how the bones in the wings of birds
are as fragile as the skim of first frost
on pasture grass – early morning,
late August.

Womb

There is always a room we will never return to.
A room shared with a lover in another country.
I come to you at night with few belongings, through moon-
blank faces. In the pace of Nevsky Prospect,
the infinity of orbit.
Turn the corner.

On the steps of the cathedral that held Dostoevsky, a man
without shoes, charred-dove feet bound in potato sacks.
Turn the corner. Shared breath of train station; snow
exhaling earth, oil, what we leave behind
in our steps, longing for home.

A kitchen – the inside smell of yeast, a tent of sleep, our bodies
when they are animal; sweat gathered where we bend.
Rye bread, wine, tea. Light a candle. Your head in my lap.
In the river-curl of your hair, slow-tongues of city-light and smoke.
Turn the corner for home.

Northern River, Tom Thomson, c. 1914–1915[2]

oil on canvas, 155 x 102 cm, National Gallery of Canada

---

2 Night moved across you like a glacier and you woke here, bone-broken, far from where you thought you would be. If you could tie a string to your what-ifs, this is what they would weave – a hydra-nest of jackpine. The way out of drowning in the foreground is a matter of perspective. You will never read all there is in the pine shadow, the dim library of your past. Look through.

Lay aside thinking. Crouch in old blood-stiff sun, moon-ash moss, the thick pelt grief grows. Crouch in the residue of snow, last season's estrus, bark, leaves; melting, a shoot of light in a winter cellar. Wear your past, a pine-shadow mane, across your back. Let your stare be a reaching hand starred with grain. Let the river come to you.

The sudden sound of your name linked to no one's, heavy as a bird without wings. Tie a string to your what-ifs. This is what they weave – the helix of your pace, a search for certainty, for a dead thing. Choose to love the living. The river is a sweating bone new from the unlit hut of the body; the river is generous, fresh-meated with reflection, balm for forest-bruised feet. Let stiff-back jackpine strip the dross of your stare, your stare a whetted reed. Song will lift from your looking.

Tantramar

At night you'd lie down beside me;
my body's drift to yours like water, a drawn reflex.
In the morning I'd bring you tea; you'd tell me fine waves of words
I murmured, thin shine of my unfocused eyes.
Crescent of iris through pleats of night,
moon in the tantramar of dream.

I thought that I was through with you.
But tonight, sitting by a man, slow static of his hand
in his beard, sound that ends in smoke, my body's drift
to you something I can't control. Your memory
on me, thin shine, unfocused eye,
moon in the tantramar of dream.

Notes towards a love poem

i

The night you held my face in your hands, your eyes were the worn metal colour of clouds heavy with snow. In your eyes I could see the season turning.

ii

Everyone has advice. Sarah says, 'Dance wildly, but try to keep one foot firmly balanced on the earth.' Though I don't say, 'I'm afraid this will only make me trip.' And I wonder – what would this look like if we weren't so cautious?

iii

Because my favourite poet, the recluse I told you about, had a lover who, before she was certain they would be together, bought a bed that she knew would fit the length of his body.

iv

Maybe what's needed is a recipe. Or potion. The kind my sister and I used to stew in old mason jars: yarrow, dandelions, spear grass, water from the rain barrel, July sun. We were just kids, though; magic was possible.

v

Later your eyes were the green of morning frost on pasture grass. They reminded me of his in which I first learned to steady my gaze.

vi

What can I give you? When first snow falls in the predawn hush, softly as moth wings closing, softly as the departure of last night's dreams, the crooked stitches of my grandmother's hand, the quilt-heat of breath, unruly hair, my flushed cheeks, hands here and here, the tender flesh and warmth of my inner thigh. The one high note in 'How Great Thou Art', which contains both how to come undone and the path back.

vii

Because my favourite poet's lover knew for certain all along.

viii

I should've shown you my heart earlier, but I was embarrassed by how it was dressed in the torn and washed-out cotton of the poor – detritus of last season's poplar leaves and bark. So instead I got drunk. Spoke out of turn. Insulted your friend. Ignored you. I know. I'm not so good at this.

ix

Because I can't help but wonder what colour your eyes are right now as I listen to the passing cars and the low hiss of night rain on the city streets.

x

I haven't written a love poem for years. I don't know if that's what this is. But I want you to tell me your sorrow. And for you to listen to mine. I wish I could sing you all the songs I know – loudly, off-key, and without shame.

xi

What can I give you? Fiery death of leaves. Deer on a sand bar, the sickle shadows of their bodies on the slowing river. A hot bowl of soup for you to thaw your cold and work-chapped hands against. Root cellar musk of onion, carrots, pepper.

xii

The more I want to show you, the further away you become. Just try to touch the horizon.

xiii

Because the story you told me about your grandfather – how, before the Russians captured him in Greece, he buried beneath a tree his wedding ring and locket, the small, sepia photo of his wife's face.

xiv

Everyone has advice. I know, I know; what I want to believe and the way things are seldom match up. I guess I didn't realize when my fortune cookie read, 'your romantic obsessions will come true' that this could mean so many different things.

xv

What's needed is a recipe. Or potion. Outside the glow of the dance hall – breath, cologned-sweat, beer, your hand on my leg while you sing Elvis songs in my ear, the prairie's last gasp of nettle and sage, 'love me tender, love me true', and if they could sing along, the stars would sound like crickets.

xvi

'Look,' I say, 'all's I know is that falling in love, or whatever this is, well, it's always a logistical nightmare.' But even as I speak, I know I'll go home to the empty cupboards of uncertainty and old mail. I'll drive too fast to beat the low sky, and though autumn has been exhaling all along, the sudden shift of light to winter will wind me.

xvii

The next day we have an awkward conversation on the patio of some bar. All elbows and sawdust tongues. I tear apart fallen elm leaves at their seams. You pull a parched flake of leaf from my hair. You love me.

xviii

A recipe. A potion. Something. The rain outside Muenster bar clinging like wet wool. The Weisner boy's worthless and sodden crops. Look south and then east. Beyond that stand of evergreens. See the porch light tunneling through damp night? That's where my father farmed his whole life. That's where I learned that sometimes there's no choice but to leave.

xix

You love me not.

xx

Because on the car-ride that day when you pointed to the magpies
teasing currents of air with tail-feathers the blue beginning of
flame, the erratic lift and fall of their glide reminded me of my
heart at recognizing the length of your forearm, your one silver
hair.

xxi

What can I give you? Funeral pyre of burning stubble, damp grass,
leaves, but then sweet smoke and ash, the rich, black earth of
my heart. All I ask in return: if you notice in the dashboard light
that my hair has fallen in my eyes, that you might hold it briefly
between your fingers, smooth it behind my ear and then linger
there.

Unsent Letter #28

Sarah, tonight a horse-hair moon. A frayed bow cricket-rubbing
against the dark string of night. A song of balance that you can
only hear if you forget that you can't.

Remember what I had said to you? That trust, like stepping off a
mountain—

But Sarah, your name reminds me that many years ago, or once
upon a time… or maybe I should introduce this differently.
Maybe these stories are the dark strings that the eye catches in old
movies – the ones we're not supposed to see. The ones that pull.

Though you were in your late nineties, you believed. Inside, your
bones shone with new fire, poplars glutted on dawn sun. And
another thing –

a stone-curlew, crow-sized, but dustier, always shamelessly singing its name, got sucked into trade winds and was forced to ride across the Atlantic on an empty stomach,

made it to southeastern Spain, the Iberian woodlands: lavender, thyme, oleander, lotus. They found him beneath a lone juniper, wind-burnt, smoking Spanish sage and whistling. Sarah, I ask you such impossible questions –

the great thing about trust, you said, is that its mystery is so much more interesting than knowing. Who can say if God will give you a child? Or that the stone-curlew, high and singing, will take the next train back?

But the bow will drop and when I hear it, the dark note of night will give me that heart-in-the-throat hover of stepping-off. So stop thinking. Hold my hand. Remember, our bones are sated light.

Nocturne

i

His voice -
whisky leaves of dusk
birch, cigarette smoke,
an e-minor guitar chord.
Caressing the night-
lake, breath and
call of a loon.

ii

When they tell me about my eyes *(green of*
frost on lake's slowing,

I say they are my father's,
pine smoke and

and when I am old
wolves under November's

they will turn blue.
Thistle-tine moon).

iii

How we fall ~
watching him
split wood,

axe over shoulder,
down the grain of
what joins us.

Wolverine Creek

Fall. When scraped fields
show us the empty-
cathedral air inside us.

Shrew sounds of leaves,
bleeding at a pace the eye can't hold.
As a child standing in willow kindle,

grasses the yellow of grandma's dying arms,
watching geese harrow a sky made
more blue by the radiance of decay,

asking for a sign –
if you are there, spell this
in the furrow of geese –

and always unable to decode
their flight, to find the equation, a basket
to heap meaning, grandma's apron full of chokecherries,

small questions, *why in death the smell of estrus?*
But soon the geese over Wolverine,
the creek that dog-legs our land.

Standing in their wake,
mind made small by another's height,
left with the imprecision of loss –

strewn chokecherries, their bee-sting
taste. Learning we reckon only through
loss: the place where we begin.

Hysterectomy

My mother's head in my lap.
She's crying. Her shirt twists up
beneath her breasts. I trace her
stretch marks, last sun

through bare birch, drifts of fallen
poppy petals at the garden's edge.
Geese knife the sky, dusk,
their cries, rusted
hinges. Listen –

winter is a door slowly closing. In the garden,
the poppy's seed pod: cured skull,
my mother's uterus, full
of dried bees.
I trace her

stretch marks, last sun, bare
birch, white of an empty bowl.
Drink her absence,
undivided
light.

Bread, Water

From the well to the porch, the nervous rasp
of boots when snow is clenched tight as glass.

Water to do the day's washing and baking. Look in.
If you can see yourself inside the pocked metal pail,

you understand – water shows you
who and where you are:

faint stars; moon, a pearl
of salt down your brow.

Words, like water, are shaped by gravity
if you can think of gravity as another way of saying

memory. Just as river wearing an elbow-worn coat
of last season's shells and leaves, makes its way

to the ocean, bread is this woman,
before dawn, making enough

for the week. Is the ripple of her muscles
kneading the belly of dough.

Sigh of yeast as she folds each loaf.
Poplar-snap in the wood-stove. Steam melting

fronds of window-frost. Aerial-
pitch of stars, pearl-of-sweat

moon. The word bread,
an estuary. Where tide gathers river,

an old friend, into its arms, pulls it
into heave and the familiar smell of salt.

Bread. Welcome.

St Benedict's Rule

You make tea for a man who was your lover.
Where once there was desire, now a palm-sized heartbeat,
pleasant to hold. Open wings of frost on the window.

He waits at a table the colour of old teeth.
Outside the abbey's kitchen (a kill-deer's nest
in fescue) a blizzard has cried itself to sleep.

Snowdrifts, wide-eyed, torn, at the corners of doors.
Whisper-light of lamp, soft-furred shadow,
metronome-breath of sleep.

You feel the thread of his gaze weave
a tapestry of the ablution you are
performing for him:

the kettle's lost key rattle,
steam, words you murmur
when you think no one is looking.

Bark and flower steeping in veined
Wheat Pool mugs. All scraps of shed clothes
from a grandmother's rag-bag, the smell of farm-

chapped hands, diesel, cured clover,
still in her worn poplin, in his worn flannel.
Once he was your lover,

he lived in a cabin on the border
of the abbey's halo. After vespers you'd go
to him. Stars, eyes of birch craning into night.

Wind in evergreens,
a lucid dream, Wolverine Creek
untethered from gravity by sleep.

He lit stubs of old altar candles, showed you how
to play guitar. Spice of his hair as he knelt before you:
beeswax, wool, smoke.

Moon, a blade sharpened so many times its light's grown soft.
The care he took: willow-balm for feet and hair,
each button undone, each finger warmed beneath his tongue.

Legato

On the hike down
Tunnel Mountain, creeping-
juniper, wet-eyed berries.

•

Under willow shrub
or larch, the white-crowned sparrow.
What I look for and what in brief moments
approaches, never match up.

•

Though they've been there all along,
bow down to the bowing crocus, lobed petals,
spring-snow blue, blue of thaw,
lucent.

•

It was after dinner. Full of the usual sadness, the world
is dying, I just wanted to go to bed. Last breath of dusk,
sun behind the erratic mountain-horizon –
held by a nameless night.

•

White-Crowned Sparrow legato: breath
through his bottom teeth and beard.

•

He was in shadow singing
the blues. Surprising lift of his voice,
flight from larch, levity of my heart in my throat.

•

Step out.
A black-billed magpie stabs
at bread left on a balcony.

•

Tail feathers: struck-match-
blue and then green
and then blue.

•

Outside of the ridiculous divisions
of time, Mount Rundle, open-eyed,
mute.

•

When my looking crumbles, rip-rap, the world appears
in fissures. White-crowned sparrow nest, a sipping-cup:
mud, lichens, shred bark, red fescue, leaves.

•

I think I've known him for at least a hundred years.
His song, honeyed unction. I think I've known him
for at least two thousand years.

•

Song contains us in a light so particular it can't be named –
crocus, struck-match-blue of magpie and then
green and then blue, juniper.

•

In-between-heartbeat brief; when I step out
of my narrow lament; when
the world looks back –

The Breath of Looking

i

The great horned owl underfeather you found
suspended on brome teaches you about the near
imperceptibility of grief. About thinness.
How light, hardly snared by down,
filters through and changes just-so
and so grief wears you, makes
you its slight shadow.

ii

The great horned owl underfeather teaches you
about the eyes of someone you long for. How if they could
stroke you, they would be as graceful as the almost
weightless. How if you could look at the sky
through them, you would feel smaller,
but not less.

iii

The great horned owl teaches you that the knack for
flight has something to do with silence. Its wings polish
planes of air; distance shimmers in their wake.
In the weeping hearts of poplar leaves,
how to feel the silk breath
of looking.

Amber

A glass of water, a prayer, a lamp left on.
Behind closed eyes, scars of light –

St Petersburg from the height of *Kazanski Sabor*.
In sun-thick snow, linen strung between windows
of jaundiced apartments, frozen sheets, empty shells

of wind. Alleys, as palm-veins, paths
to hidden doors. You gave me an amber
stone, memory of spring. My face fixed

against your chest in *Letniy Sad*,
we read in the watery shine
of new leaves.

I wake in forgotten light
to loosened blood.

Unsent Letter #47

Gray nap of false dawn held in the glass of water I left beside the lamp the night before. It's May. The moment in bed before we rise, when dream has not yet given way to what we can bite into. Or a thin taper – skittish flame and, in any breath, only the smoke-tail of some burrowing animal.

The trick of May is to believe with empty hands. And then always, after we fail at faith, small-fires of crocus or bluebell snag the eye. But Cory, it's been raining for weeks and

elms are old men sitting on the porch of the local hotel. Cartilage-worn, they hum country songs of bone on bone. This is all there is. You told me once that sky in the May of your childhood, Grenfell, south of Regina, is the colour of your old blue t-shirt. Maybe someone has said it better, you thought. Maybe not.

Somewhere I read that Renoir believed what survives the artist is the feeling he gives through objects. This morning, stretched across its heart, sky wears a t-shirt rubbed butterfly-thin by so many slow Saturday mornings, coffee and a newspaper, sleep-thick limbs.

Cory, it's been raining for weeks, but as I write this two boys throw a tennis ball at a garage door. Small-fire pulse of sun at the corner of the eye. This is all there is. I have traveled for a season and at the end of my hunger, who could imagine

such abundance! A last swallow of cold coffee, the slap of boy-shouts and a ball. Sky, old-t-shirt blue, woven of so many petals of rain.

That Song That Goes

For no reason I can name
I look away from the book and see
the moon deepen into golds and reds.
Eastern sky a sodden blue. Spring
dusk is something to breathe deeply –
wet dirt, stubble, last year's leaves.
And like a dream that comes back
only when unasked for, I recall
his hands from when I was a child –
rough wood, tobacco, metal of earth.
A friend tells me of early grey mornings
at his kitchen table. There was tea,
the beginnings of a wood-fire, his wife,
bread. And the winter riverbed, the long,
slow ache I carry inside, briefly fills

with the singing of Spring melt.
Memory is that song the heart hums
along with. The one without
thinking, beneath breath.

Come

I will follow you, I said, to a place where night is a season,
where the horizon is as fine as, beneath a lover's hand,
lacing on a chemise. I will follow you to a city sewn by river,
where we'll stand on a canal, your hands warming in my coat,
horizon open, our faces in a constellation of snow and stars.
I will follow you to where there is no parting, to a city
sewn by river, horizon spilling snow, spilling stars,
your hands warming in my coat, near a river,
for a season, for an hour.

Come, you said,

Come.

wait. My grandfather's crop is in so my dad can work road crew. Sixteen hour days driving grader. Saving eight bucks an hour to buy his own place. NW 18 36 22 W2nd. A name that will mark distance. But now, I imagine him humming small-songs that mean home:

work boots by a door; kitchen window frost; honey and tea; his hands unclenching against her breasts; stars. I've never really listened to his stories so

I don't know where he is, but July sun, a whetstone, thins his body. Later scars of heat sweat clay splintered trees are totem to what breaks him. His eyes, the colour of a palmed drink from slough.

After, he'll drink whisky, woman-hand warm, to *sshh* away the many-million insect shriek of machine. To ease his bones into the camp's plywood bunk-bed: hot cup, night- window, his hands, her breasts, stars. He is mad with grief, but

no one believes him. I've never listened to his stories, but there is no time for shame. Someone has thrown me in front of his blade. Throat, bare-mirror in sun. *Quick!* I'll be ground into soil. Ash, smoke of an old war. My heart, clipped-

tongue, caws for air. *Quick!*

Somewhere a man digs dirt in heat. Sweat, clay, splinters, leaves in his hair. Plough on rock. He knows there will be ash, smoke. Woman-hands. Whisky. Shriek of machine. And after that his name will mark distance. It'll break him,

but no one believes. He is mad with grief. Why does he stop ploughing? Jump off the grader? Wipe dirt from my eyes? By my name he gives up so much. *Sshh.* There is no time for shame. *Now*

Notes to *Thin Moon Psalm*

Lastochka makes reference to the 900 day siege of St Petersburg by Nazi Germany. On 8 September 1941, the Germans fully encircled St Petersburg and the siege began. It lasted until 27 January 1944.

Palace Square: originally the palace of tsar Peter the Great that overlooks the Neva, now a museum called the Hermitage. The square is a centre for city gatherings.

Shostakovich: Russian composer, Dmitri Shostakovich (1906–1975).

Čiurlionis: Lithuanian artist and composer, Mikalojus Konstantinas Čiurlionis (1875–1911).

Ge: Russian painter, Nikolai Ge (1831–1894).

Kazanski Sabor: Kazan Cathedral, St Petersburg, Russia.

Letniy Sad: Summer Garden, a park of Peter the Great's that faces the Neva.

New Poems

Slaughter

I thought there'd always be a lustre of time,
rich and slick like the animal's oiled hide. I shot one

for its leather, another for the tender meat of its spine.
One more for the fetor of estrus in fur, for its tree-rubbed horns,

the spice of cedar and pine. One for its muscled gallop,
the crack and the echo, the arc of the bullet shattering prairie night.

For the shocked silence after the last steamed snort and cry. I stood
high on a pile of bones, sun-sucked skulls, rifle erect at my side.

From a thicket of poplar and birch, the coyotes' keen rose,
cut through industry's metallic reek, shroud of gunsmoke.

Drunk and glutted, sweet grease on my lips, I never thought
that my careless slaughter would lead to such hunger –

thin hospital flannel wrapped around my shoulders
by some kind nurse – that I'd be here,

trying to atone for that wasted flesh,
keeping vigil at your bedside.

Nativity

After it all, November sky
over our razed fields,

a boiled bone, a bloodless lung.
Flax stubble, ash and spent wicks.

Thin smoke in the middle distance,
as though harvest was a war –

at thaw the armor will roll out, dig in,
begin again. But then the bluing eastern horizon,

sheen on worn iron, and suddenly snow fell.
Hip-high drifts blown against the garden fence.

You wanted to walk outside so I found our winter coats
in the basement closet, still holding our shape.

I thought of matted pasture grass
where a deer has lain. Sleeping

spoor of the body woven into wool –
dust, old hair, sweat, cologne. In the snow

we were made new. Snow, a cool chrism
on last season's wounds. You laughed

as a child can, unburdened,
mouth open, face to sky,

snow melting on your tongue.
Head shorn from surgery,

in your brown coat you looked like a happy monk,
so I joined you. Dizzy with praise and falling

snow, we sank to our knees, rose
again into the frosted clouds of our breath,

and breathed in those small ghosts
of who we were just moments before.

Rise When You Hear

Without light, we have
no sense of up or down,
says my father's friend, a miner. Miles underground,

he feels like he's rising and plunging
at once. His first time below, he fell to his knees,
pressed his cheek to a night-sky of dirt.

On the hour, an ICU nurse hollers
into your ear, the shaft to a cave
where you huddle, broken-limbed, lost.

Rise when you hear your name,
a torch to orient you,
hands to break your fall.

Alms

I held your hand when the doctor spoke
for fear that your touch was the last I'd feel
before the weather cools – your life
falling from you plain as leaves
from the poplars that shelter our farm.
Hungry, wearing borrowed clothes,
after the doctor left, I crouched in a stairwell.
My eyes, green gloss on a copper begging-bowl.
Most hurried past. A few did not turn away.
Alms, simple food, bright coin of their gaze.

Gone

Blood wells in your brain and loosens the seams of time: memory is like those worn patches of cloth you quilted to keep your babies warm. Ninety-three, you fell outside your apartment door. Now Carol, your youngest, is the baby you brought home from St Elizabeth's hospital to die. And you scold my dad. Thirteen again, drunk on dandelion wine, he's singing Catholic hymns in German while playing that accordion you ordered from Eaton's.

You were born in the side of a hill. Carmel, Saskatchewan – named for Our Lady by the Benedictine monks who arrived just before. Hollowed out and covered with sod, that first winter your mother cried – no place to hang the lace curtains. Kerosene and cold dirt, the sleeping breath of wild onion. She cried for the one who didn't make it across. For the stone splash of her unbaptized body as it slipped into the sea. Agnes forever rootless and now the rest of you buried in a strange soil, weeds.

My mother had a dream before your fall – my sister and I took you back to the farm. You wept at the kitchen table. *We held her,* mom said, *and promised to take her home. There was the smell of burning poplar; you girls were making bread.*

I watch Dad hold your hands. His face loosens, scars undone. It's not implausible – thirteen. He's scared to become an orphan. The strings in his chest so tight, the one relief is the keen they make in the wind so he sings you an old Marian hymn. I recognize the words, but they're not a rich earth where I can stake claim. The farm, sold, and our blue spruce, their sleek shadows all we knew of water on skin during those years of drought, are dying too.

When I was born you made me a quilt – red paisley from a Christmas tablecloth, purple vetch patterned on a thin house-dress yellowed from decades of your body's salt. And at nineteen, when I left for good, you made me another. Kept warm in foreign countries by the stitches of your hands, I didn't know that I'd never be able to return, or that when I did, I'd feel more lost than when I was away.

You want to feel the sun on your face; we wrap your legs in a hospital blanket, tuck you into a wheelchair. Light through the first green flush of aspen leaves is the colour of your husband's eyes. When you die you'll be buried alongside him in a graveyard lined with evergreens. Like that copse of spruce he planted around the farmyard after he left the priesthood and you married. Maybe the spruce reminded him of dark forests from the stories of his youth. But they don't belong on the dry prairie. You had to water them every day, coax them to take root.

I wish I could return you to that hill of your birth, to the shaggy pelt of a pasture – only prickly rose, brown-eyed susans, buffalo beans, and the note of a western meadowlark to sing your burying.

The door of a woodstove cracked open, spring wind blasts us – the smell of birch sap, dirt knived open for seed. When Dad leans over to see if you're okay, you whisper to him about the wind bending the branches of evergreens. He smiles at me, but I remember Mom's dream. You were already in that kitchen where Dad sang his songs, where you brought Carol back to life, where from the window you could watch night gathering beneath spruce. But still you wept as your mother wept. For the room in the hill. For the lace curtains. For what's torn apart at the seams. Our roots here too thin, promises we couldn't keep. Umbilicus ripped, we're drifting unbaptized in a place we poured our lives into, where we fell short of learning how to be.

Magnificat

Magnificat anima mea Dominum

You thought there'd be an emissary.
Dawn grey feathers and webbing
pressed against the care home window.
Like in that sepia story –

your sister, the Spanish flu. Coal-eyed,
ripe with fever, bound in sweat's tight lace,
she begged for an open window,
though January prairie, a knife
held to the throat.

Last deep swallow of frost, milk-blue
shadows of snow, and she gave up the ghost,
you told us with the conviction of your faith,
just crosshairs away from superstition.

She's buried in that abandoned cemetery,
St Scholastica's, northwest of the farm.
After supper, summer, we'd walk there
through hanks of ditch grass –

fescue, brome, spear, bluestem, blue-eyed,
hip-high sow thistle, coyote-scat cairns,
creeping smoke of pasture sage, sparrow drone.
You showed us where parishioners
peeled back the thick loam,

tucked in your nameless sisters. No stones
to mark graves, but a wind-gnawed cross,
prickly rose budding in sun-cured cow shit,
tiger-lilies, lit flares. Oldest daughter,
you prepared them for the earth,

wiped vernix from fists and eyes. Fetal curled,
washed clean of birth's grease, sebum and cilia,
like the vegetable seeds you steeped to soften husks.
Their infant skulls, allium bulbs, pulp rich and sweet
with utero-dreams of silver light in birch leaves,
of grasses' low suss.

On our walk home, a creek-cool breeze sliced the dusk-
perfume of flowering canola, yellow blooms electric
in the black light of a thunderstorm, kick and snort
of horses penned, mounting on the horizon.

No flash of grief as you stood on the soil
of your sisters, their fine ribs stripped
of marrow and sap, plaited by dirt
into almsbaskets, heirloom pearl.

Plainsong

Driving home from Uncle Richard's,
in the backseat with my brother and sister –
weft of limbs, pearlescence of moonlit skin,
shift and fall of their breath.

My face against the car window to watch stars, and every mile
a farm, yard-lights,
a voice in plainsong –

after feeding the cattle, Dave Saretsky stepping into his porch,
borscht warming on the stove,
hambone, pepper, cloves.
She›s tucking in their youngest boy,
her palm on his feverish cheek.
After, she and Dave will sleep, in the space their bodies have
learned
to make from years of sharing
blood, spit, loam –

Blink of frost on wheat stalks, fields left in stubble to snare
October›s first snow-squall, the tip of dad›s
cigarette,
knots of smoke, mother singing low to the radio,
the gypsy-light of stars and farms,
a raw harmony

like the dark wave of geese lifting off the slough just east of
our barns.
Their winter homing, a folksong for the journey
to where flesh might belong.

Our farm's sold. Dave's too. Uncle Richard died seventeen years ago.
Only now the light of this memory reaches me. Its
source, gone

Feast

Chokecherries, spider webs,
slough water spiced with lilac,
spear grass, cattails, caragana pods.
Farm debt. Drought. The locust drone
of adult-talk. *Girls, come in for lunch.*
Ignore mom's cries. Rhubarb stalks
dipped in stolen sugar. Shelled peas,
carrots from the garden, dirt shaken off.
Our table set in the smolder of sage,
the river scent of wolf willow shade.
Our feast made sweet by loss.

Silence

to A. S.

'The moment stands still. The whole of space is filled [...] with a dense silence which is not absence;[...] it is the secret word, the word of Love who holds us [...] from the beginning.'

Simone Weil, letter to Joë Bousquet, 1942

You ask me what kind of silence the moon makes
as I stand at my kitchen window watching the August moon

gather into its apron wings of mist from the lake.
Swathed in dusk incense – balsam, reed grass, cricket hum,

the moon is a henna stained palm, cupped.
I haven't answered your question. Can I find it in my body?

Yours is in the marsh of your chest, red-winged black bird
nesting in prairie sedge. Inside me, behind the oak doors of hips,

Rembrandt-lit, a wine-ringed table, broken bread. Someone was there
and left. But this room isn't empty, is it. Full of the silence

you've shown me. Moon rising over lake.
Cattails, flare of wings. Guttering light in a wine glass.

Near the Saskatchewan River

Three years later, you see her. The child who called *Mama!*
every day, late afternoon. Her voice rose in the courtyard

beneath your bedroom window – first snow, pigeon down,
wet newsprint, and the oil-stain of night seeping over the embankment

of the Neva. *Mama!* and you look up from where you sit now,
near the Saskatchewan River, its hills like the flanks of running horses.

Grasses pared by summer's last heat. Between your fingers
you roll chokecherries, blood-shot pouches of skin

beneath tired eyes. The dusk moon, exhaled breath
of a whitetail, is snagged on aspens, *Mama!* and you watch

her run down steps, two at a time, into her mother's arms.
You feel her small body, the warm heave of her chest

as she leans into her mother's thighs like that moth-flutter
pulse you once held inside. *Mama!* Chokecherry pulp

has stained your fingers red, and as you walk away,
the moon in the aspens loosens, lets go.

Dusk

Hyacinth petals, wet, on cobblestone.
Late afternoon. Smell of burning oil. Rain
pitching a tent of night, I thought of you.

After the parade, streamers and beads strewn down the close.
In a doorway a man smokes a cigar. The echo of drums
turned my heart into a bruise, at the back of my throat,
the taste of burning oil.

Remember that hungry-eyed child, her mother barefoot,
who watched as we waited for the train in Moscow?
Our love so decadent, a mouthful of meat,
my stomach turned when she begged for food
in the stations' stench of burning oil.

Now Edinburgh's tenements, darkened by coal smoke, remind me
of you – how you came home to our flat with black bread and fruit,
the candlelight through our kitchen window
glowed at dusk like burning oil.

By the position of its stars, the Elsheimer painting can be dated
1609, late June. I'm stunned by a longing so precise, by a lake
lit by moon, its sheen the colour of burning oil.

Night and the Silence

Morning light through my attic window
holds in its bird-bone palm the jar I filled with azalea petals,
and like Orpheus I find myself trying to sing that love is plain.

But remember the moon last night? Stalactite-thin,
thin as the name, Eurydice. One star, a tear on night's limestone
throat.
She knows his songs for her were just his way of watching himself,

trying to avoid what we all try to avoid –
what is exceeds its names, petals bright as open mouths;
light is too simple; love has more to do with shadow, our failure to
reach.

Mandatum Novum

How you find me: moon,
rough-woven osier, unravels.
Night sky, blood when it is still

held in our bodies. Stars
chide in a foreign language
and I'm back at a market

in St Petersburg. Hungry,
I try to say bread, but am berated
by words I can't enter.

Sitting on steps, mute under stars,
hungry and looking away:
how you find me.

Moon undone, you kneel.
Though I might be the one
who will betray you,

you reach in that dark, pull me
to the thrum of your heart,
slide off my stockings.

Savannah Sparrow

i

How a voice can measure your ear,
wave filling ribbed sand.
In the static of crickets,
a grassy hiss.

ii

The breast-arch of sparrow
shows you how your hip
would feel to the hand
that is absent.

iii

Sparrow song comes
by such fine degrees, it stuns.
The wild roses this morning,
pursed lips, now a burst of song.

Hopewell, New Brunswick

When the tide is out, you take me to the mud-flats at Hopewell.
A fault pulled this section of shore apart. Sandstone cliffs, cracked ribs –
hawkweed, feldspar, raven feathers, quartz.

We wade through clay, iron oxide, exposed blood.
On your knees, you show me what I thought was the glyph of a wing,
but is evidence of a nephtys' passing.

Like when we speak of the heart – not flight, but a trace fossil,
imprint of bodies slipped away. Cut by high-tide, we can't go back.
Torn quilt of white pine, north sky churns snow.

Spring Rain, Glasgow

Rain, late spring sings *only this, only this,*
stirs the scent of spear thistle, willowherb,
the wych elm's rising sap, Glasgow's undertones,
oil, wet sandstone, street-dirt. I listen as though
I might hear something to explain last winter
when sky wore the pallor of cigarette smoke,
ash. Rain falls without answers or portents.
I listen as though it might imply forgiveness –
            bud husk, croci,
                        juniper, mown grass.

Early Spring, Dancing

When he holds her fingertips,
I think of the ripe tulips on my kitchen sill,

sugars rising to the heat of touch,
petals flushed as our bodies after love.

How long since I've turned my face
to the blue spring sky?

Ballast

I dreamt about him again, a man I barely know,
lace of first snow on his shoulders. I reach to hold him,
to brush away that fine burden and pull him from a day-after-day
winter that is coming. A man I barely know, but love

for the stories he told me as we drove through dusk. October air,
honey rimed with the Atlantic's breath. Auxin thinning in the leaves,
beeches and maples, Nova Scotia's white aspens. Branches, wicks
for the gutter of carotene, cinnabar, burnt-blood, the bright death
they bore all summer laid bare by the season's vagrant light.

After the sun burrowed into the nap of the woods,
shed fur and boughs, the kindling of a lantern-lit barn
or distant flicker of Sackville, then Truro, gave rise to a stray
dog, fox, a skim of migrating thrush. Nameless shadows,
muddy patina on the violet of new night.

I'd catch a ride with him to Antigonish so I could stay with a friend.
It was the drive I waited for all week. Hearth of his car radio,
jazz I'd never heard, whisky-toned horns wandering like ghosts
of all the selves he wore until deep into an evening, years ago,
he held open a library door for her. In that first gust of Hamilton dark,

smelt iron, stars, Lake Ontario silt, he said he knew
their whole life together was furled. Pressed by years into ritual,
the fires he lit for her Saturday mornings in predawn fog, coffee, toast,
kettle purring on the stove, bergamot-steam, lapping breath of
their sons'
hungry slumber, her uncombed hair, animal musk of sleep.

When the gleam of that dulls, empties into habit,
when you think you know her in your bed, fling open the window.
Look again, he said. The clear taste of her skin, sweet clover, dried sea,
fined by crushed eggshells, pearls of first light. Like her glass of wine

in that obituary photo announcing her death.
Warmed by her palms in the resin of after-supper sun,
her syrah held the spice of sap, sugar, flame, spinning leaves.

His stories – he held her like that, turned the crimson gem over in
his hands,
saying the thousand names for that late summer blaze.

Once, part way to Fredericton, he realized he'd forgotten his wallet,
so we drove back. He invited me in – knitting slumped by a woodpile,
books on a kitchen sill, their youngest, struck shy by my intrusion,
clung to his knees. She knew he couldn't, still she asked him
to stay another night, lessen the distance of the work week.

When he hugged her goodbye, I felt their close breath.
There's hunger, but then there's hunger
too in the presence of bread you can't have.
She set a place for me, a stranger at their table. I left sated,

like last summer, watching my mother
quiet my newborn niece. In the hover of July heat,
a vanishing contrail of memory – how it felt to be swathed in her
low songs and sway, lilac talc, pasture sage. We are so fragile
and die from happenstance. Cells flower, a vein bursts.

One minute my mother smoothes chaff from my hair, thunderclouds
blooming west of our farm. The next, she lies in an ambulance.
My dreams of him a rehearsal, yet I wake left with nothing –
I'm sorry for your loss. You're in my prayers. –
those turned-out-pocket phrases.

We have no choice. We say yes to the deaths we contain. Ballasts,
otherwise the moments between are too fine – before the weather
breaks, slack curls of breeze, shadows of poplars' shivering hearts
in my eyes, lilac, my mother's hands, sage freed by sudden rain.

Vigil

to Yi-Mei Tsiang

I am no longer young. I know
what we love we will lose.
Your head resting in my lap
as you hold your newborn
to your open breasts, milk scent,
mown hay. Snow falls
beneath the street lamp's glow,
flutter of her eyelashes as you nurse
her into dreams of light and shadow.
I read in the tow of candles we lit
to mark this evening's coming.
With my free hand I gloss dark waves
of your hair. All I want is to unknot
what anchors you here, to ease you
into sleep. If I could read the notes
of your new mother's heartbeat
I feel against my thighs,
they'd be a lullaby –
Don't be afraid.
We love what we will lose.
I am not young anymore.
Your body sighs, you slip
into sleep's undertow,
the anchor rope
tossed to shore.

Acknowledgements

Poems from *Earth After Rain* first appeared as an award-winning publication by Thistledown Press.

Poems from *Thin Moon Psalm* reprinted courtesy of Brick Books.

Thanks to friends and to past editors of the poems: Dianne Chisholm, Christine Ferguson, Warren Heiti, Tim Lilburn, Tim McIntyre, Don McKay, Anne Simpson, John Steffler, Sharon Thesen and, of course, Sarah Tsiang.

Thanks to everyone at Carcanet Press, Brick Books, and Thistledown Press.

Thank you Michael Schmidt. Working with you is a great joy.

Thanks to the literary journals in which these poems first appeared, most recently *PN Review*, *Riddle Fence*, *The Fiddlehead*, *Event*, and *Grain*.

Thanks to the Saskatchewan Arts Board for providing support.

Thank you Rosalie, Larry, Kurt, and Heather Benning, and the Duncans.

And to Fraser, my love. (Ruth 1:16)